Selling My Home
With Regina Pope

Compiled By:
Douglas A Franklin

Copyright © 2024 Douglas A Franklin

All rights reserved.

ISBN: 9798339194255

DEDICATION

Hi, I'm Regina and I'm super happy to dedicate this book to you! We covered a lot of common questions that friends like you have experienced over the years. This keepsake book is just for you, and I look forward to working with you and your family for many years to come!

CONTENTS

	Acknowledgments	i
0	Introduction	Pg #3
1	Awards & Certificates	Pg #5
2	Referrals & References	Pg #8
3	How Should I Price My Home	Pg #10
4	How You Plan To Market My Home	Pg #18
5	What Can I Do To Increase My Home's Value	Pg #27
6	What Are The Costs Associated With Selling My Home	Pg #37
7	How Long Sales Typically Take	Pg #47
8	What Should I Expect During The Sales Process	Pg #57

9	What Are The Potential Risks & Challenges	Pg #62
10	Strong Process To Vet Buyers	Pg #71
11	How Do You Handle Offers & Negotiations	Pg #75
12	What Else Sets You Apart From Other Realtors	Pg #81
	Conclusion	Pg #91

Acknowledgments:

    I would like to deeply thank my family for all their support, and you for your interest and time talking to me as we establish and grow our friendship!

                                - Regina

Introduction:

Hi there. Today we are with Regina Pope with Shaw Real Estate in Pearland, Texas. Regina, how are you today?

Regina: "Hi, Doug. I'm doing well. How are you?"

Very good. We've known each other for about six years now, right?

Regina: "About right."

And, during that time you've been a real estate agent, so you've got a lot of experience in the industry, especially in the Houston and Pearland area, correct?

Regina: "Yes, I do."

Would you mind telling us a little bit more about that?

Regina: "Yes, absolutely.

"I've been in real estate, for quite a while now. I've been with Shaw Real Estate for four years, and I service all of the greater Houston area.

"The office is in Pearland, but I have expertise in the neighborhoods within the area within the radius. I've been in real estate, but I've been with Shaw Real Estate for four years.

"I've been the top producer for the last three consecutive years.

"I have intense knowledge in the Pearland area, Webster, Houston, Friendswood, and all the greater Houston area. I have an understanding of our local market."

1) Awards & Certificates

Excellent. If you don't mind, would you mind sharing your real estate education, and any awards and certificates you've received in the business?

Regina: "Certainly, I have the seller representation seller specialist certification, as well as I got my luxury seller certification last year when I got the Sterling Mansion listing which is a historical piece in Houston."

Would you mind being a little bit, giving us a little bit more on those two? What do those certifications entail?

Regina: "The luxury seller representative certification caters exactly to sellers and gives us in-depth knowledge on that side of the transaction and how to sell your home, how to advise, how to negotiate, and how to do.

"From start to finish to facilitate the deal to make a smooth transaction for our sellers."

And then there was a second certificate. I don't recall the exact name.

**Regina: "It was the luxury home certification last August. I was granted the listing. Correct. For the starting

mention in Houston, that is a 5.1 Million dollar mention.

"So any property that's about 1.2 Million is considered a luxury property. So there's a certification that I had to take to be able to list these properties."

What is the difference between the high-end million-plus property listings and a standard property listing that you might run into?

Regina: "Great question.

"There's not a difference.

"The only thing is you're dealing with more of the affluent lifestyle, sellers, and buyers.

"I don't know if that answers your question."

I think so.

It's definitely the same.

Regina: "The transaction is the same, the pieces are the same. The difference is that you're dealing with different types of socioeconomic individuals."

2) Referrals & References

Understood. If you don't mind let's talk about your referrals and references. Do you have any testimonials about how good your work is?

HAR.COM
Sellers Rating of Regina Pope
"Regina Pope is the most knowledgeable, experienced and comm…

Regina: "Yes, I do. I have serviced over 50 families and I've received several five-star reviews, testimonials, and also Google reviews on my HAR profile that they've been satisfied with my service.

"People I work with like that I treat

them like family versus just a transaction."

So people have gone out of their way to enroll in the Houston area realtor's website and create accounts for themselves. And then on top of that, go into the troll transaction of reviewing you there as an additional. As an additional vote of confidence in you.

Regina: "Correct."

Okay. That's excellent. If you don't mind, you're ready to dive right in.

Regina: "Yeah, let's do it."

3) How Should I Price My Home?

All right. So the first and greatest question that everybody's going to have on their minds is how should I price my home?

Regina: "Yes, great questions.

"I get that a lot.

"So to be able to price your home correctly, what we will do is conduct the

CMA. That is a comparative market analysis that assesses the homes that have sold or are very similar to our subject property.

"Now the reason for the sale is also what an appraisal, an appraiser will take into consideration. So the comps, the comparative analysis is for homes that sold within a radius. So they start within the neighborhood, we start within about a mile out, up to three miles.

"These are the same steps that an appraiser would do to look at the homes that sold are very similar in square footage location and features and benefits. Now, we don't, I don't only just focus on the soul but also focus on the active, which would be the competitive homes that are active on the market. So that'd be your competition.

"Once we determine a good price to make it very attractive, then we list it at that price to bring more qualified buyers. We have a strategy that we use at Shaw Real Estate, where we look at pricing, and then we set a price where it's a little bit below market value.

"That way we have multiple offer scenarios. Means that buyers were going to come to the property. They're going to say, Hey, I love this house. Let's put it in an offer right away.

"And then we create a multiple offer scenario where we have competitive offers and then we have multiple offers and then we drive the price up."

Okay. I think there are two major threads there that I'd like to explore. If you don't mind, let's have a quick chat about the You'd mentioned the homes in the area. So if there are, what are the conditions that your listers are going to be interested in having when they're looking for the best listing scenario for themselves?

Regina: "A lot of it is the condition of the property.

"So updates, repairs, anything they can do that they can compare themselves

to the ones that are sold. So for example, if your house is dated and the neighbor's house just sold for an amount that you may think your house is worth, but they have updates, the house can't be apples to apples.

"It would be comparable based on square footage, number of bedrooms, and lot size location, but then we would have to adjust for improvements."

Some interesting pieces in there. I believe so. There are some interesting pieces in there that I'd like to talk about a little bit more. You're saying that even though these homes can be very similar in the same neighborhoods, in the same area, just by the taste and texture of the home, you may have a completely different opinion from families coming to look at your home because you have kept updates in your home.

And you're finding that's a greater driver than a lot of other factors.

Regina: "Yeah, absolutely.

Improvements, curb appeal, repairs, and things that are attractive to a new buyer would separate your home. Each home has its unique features and benefits and we take all of that into consideration.

"When we price a home we take a tour of the property, we look at it, we measure it. We make sure that we add or subtract for any type of improvements or not improvements to the subject property."

And then you'd also brought up that as a strategy during your listing process, you would like to see multiple offers coming on the same listing. Therefore you list at a slightly lower than, Market price and allow the interested buyers to compete and improve their offer prices. Is that accurate?

Regina: "That is correct.

"We've been doing this strategy even since before coven and multiple offers for a thing. If you price the property, right, it will sell.

"We have three factors on that. We have the location, condition, and price.

"If we price it correctly, the price, the home will not be in the market too long. You won't sit there too long people are going to start wondering what happened if we price it right.

"We should have many showings and we should have many offers in the first two weeks of the property being live a thing.

"If you price the property right, it will sell. have 3 factors on that. We have the location, condition, and price.

"We should have many showings and we should have many Offers in the first two weeks of the property being live on the market if we do not have that where we have showings and offers then that means its price is too high."

Do you use any other incentives to get searching agents in to see things like offers agents offers or anything like that? Or do you?

As a matter of course, prefer to stick with a standard quality listing price and allow the agents to bring buyers to you.

Regina: "Yes. Yes, we do that also, Sellers, they ask for our expertise.

"If we price it correctly, we'll have the Buyer's agents bring the offers and we present those offers to the sellers.

"Right now, we have had sellers where they have a price in mind. And sometimes it doesn't match the comps, but at the end of the day, they're the boss. We do what they want us to do.

"We'll try it, and if we don't have offers in the first two weeks, then we go back and revisit that question.

"Go into the strategic pricing strategy that we do, marking it below market value to bring more buyers and drive the price."

Okay, so do you have anything else that you'd like to add about pricing your home?

Regina: "Every home is unique.

"And again, we like to see it and we like for it to be, like to look good, smell good, to show well, and be able to be available for showings.

"That also brings offers.

"If the home is ready to go, you could still be living in the property.

"But be flexible when it comes to showing the property, because the more it shows, the better it's going to sell."

4) How You Plan To Market My Home?

If you don't mind, let's look at how you plan to market my home when I list with you. What

are your steps that you like to go through to do the marketing process to show new, to get the most amount of eyes onto the homes that you're listing?

Regina: "Yeah, absolutely.

"So our marketing plan does include professional photography. We get photography done and drone photography for every one of our listings.

"We syndicate to all, it's on our website, and we syndicate to all of the websites, including the MLS. We do social media promotions, and we do ads

"And then we hold an open house, call and invitation mailings. The key part

here is that we call neighborhoods in the surrounding area.

"We try to find the buyers that want to move into the neighborhood. We call the neighbors, and ask, 'Hey, do you know anybody who wants to live next door to you? You can choose your neighbor.'

That's the strategy that's been helping.

"I don't think anybody's doing this. A lot of agents aren't calling.

"We call and we call a lot to find a buyer."

So let me key on that calling the neighbors because that level of follow-up is, I'm going to use the word, the overused word exceptional, because I know from my own experience when people in the sales, industry do exceedingly well in the follow-up and the calling process, you're going to have a vastly different result than someone who's passive and Is not taking care of their leads and would you mind going in a little bit more to explain how that differentiates you from all the other agents in the area.

Regina: "Yes, absolutely.

"As far as follow up that's the key.

"Just like you mentioned, calling potential buyers, and finding the potential buyers is important, because a lot of the time the MLS will do its thing, right?

"You'll list it. People will see it. That's not enough.

"That's like me waiting for a buyer to come.

"I go and find the buyer and follow up with not just the neighbors, but all the leads that come through for this property is where we can vet the new buyers that come our way. And also the interested parties.

"We treat each lead like a gold nugget to call and follow up on, we do at least 8 touches. Before we let that lead, either,

they tell us, 'Hey, I'm not interested. Don't call me again.'

"We keep it, we put it in the archive we follow up until we get an answer.

"And that could be up to 8 touches."

So this might be a little bit technical and if it's close hold information, please let me know what is in your experience. What is the difference in show length for someone who does not do that kind of intensive research and lead generation versus an agent like yourself who's doing exceptional work and advocating for your clients.

While listing your home, what is the average show duration? Is there a difference in listing prices? How do you, is that something that you've quantified?

Regina: "Not necessarily.

"I treat all my listings at any price point the same.

"The difference is a lot of agents just

list and sit there and they, like I said, don't follow up and they just wait.

"The market's been hot.

"Let's just be real.

"People will put it on the and then we'll sell because we're in such high demand and low inventory.

"In our area, especially in Houston and the greater Houston area.

"So many families are moving here, so they want to be in the area.

"However, just putting on the MLS is not enough. So this year, 2024, we've had a lot of agents put them on MLS and the property is just sitting there for a while not selling quickly.

"They're not having multiple offers. They might have 1 showing every other week. And that used to be the norm back whenever it was a buyer's market.

RECENTLY SOLD

$568,5000 — 22106 Chesterwick Dr, Katy, TX
$309,000 — 1210 Indian Autumn Trace, Houston, TX
$260,000 — 4603 Waialae Circle, Pasadena, TX

"Now we're still in a seller's market, so putting the home on MLS, it will still sell, but if you wanna sell it quickly, then you have to do that follow-up.

"I have a story, same neighborhood, two different sellers.

"One listing has been sitting there for a while. I called the agent and they had multiple open houses. Open houses just bring some buyers and some that aren't just nosy neighbors. So their listing was sitting there for over 36 days with no offers with maybe a handful of showings.

"I got the listing down the street and put it on the market.

"We had 37 showings. And we had seven offers within the first weekend of putting it live.

"I called the neighborhood. I called the neighbors. One of the neighbors was interested.

He didn't go through with it, but then we found a buyer just that was one neighborhood over.

"So what they were doing, they were trying to upgrade like, 'Hey, you're in a three bedroom. You're trying to upgrade to a four-bedroom. I have a great four-bedroom over here. Let me show you!'

"If that answers your question."

Think so. So, basically you're 11 times more

effective by doing the calls and the follow-ups because as opposed to 36 days, you worked things through and had seven offers in four days I think you said

Regina: "Yes, the weekend, and we had 37 showings, we had 7 offers, and we closed in 38 days. From the closing day, it was 38 days."

So the other house down the street sat and had nobody look at it and in that time you Had seven offers and closed the home down the street.

Regina: "That just literally happened."

That's pretty amazing Is there anything else you'd like to add to how you do marketing?

Regina: "And like I was saying, photography is key, and we can go into like, how? Giving tips on how to make the home increase in value, making it show-ready for buyers to come in and say, Hey, I like this house. I want to put in an offer. So curb appeal."

So I think that kind of segues into our next question

5) What Can I Do To Increase My Home's Value?

What can I do to increase my home's value when I'm listening to you?

Regina: "Yes, definitely.

"We want the buyers to fall in love

with your property.

"A fresh coat of paint on the front door, because remember going to drive in, park in the driveway, and the front door is going to be the main thing that they see. So it's, if you can't, that's fine, but maybe get a power wash.

"The front door and just the opening of the exterior to look very well maintained. The patio, and that fresh coat of paint for that door will make a difference.

"Adding flowers to the front porch or your flower beds, having that landscaping, making it very beautiful and vibrant flowers for the buyers to come in and just feel inviting and warm that wanted to come in. 'Hey, I can live here again, park in the driveway, see the front door see your front porch with flowers'.

"I think that's a big point and pressure washing.

"Like I said, if you can't paint, that's

okay.

"Let's get it cleaned up.

"I think that's very key.

"And also, the garage door, some people neglect that. And then sometimes in the gutters, there's stuff growing. You need to clean gutters and pressure washers, anything, the exterior that will make it look good.

"Okay. I recommend changing the light bulbs on the front porch is another good one. That way, if they are coming in the evening and the lights are on they can just see, okay it's nice and lit. We can see going up to the door and also helps with photography.

"Part of our photography package is we'll do a twilight photo and we turn the lights on from the outside pictures.

"And also maintain the lawn!

"We're in Houston, it's warm. The

lawn grows.

"**Very often, keeping that maintained while the house is on the market and while you're living there, that way it's very manicured and kept up. So it shows well.**

"**Another piece would be if you have numbers on your house.**

"**You might want to replace them or get repainted, sometimes they have curb numbers.**

"**If there is no sign and there are no numbers, or they are hard to see, buyers may have a hard time finding your house.**

"**So I recommend getting that, making it easier for them to find you and overall enhancing the curb appeal.**"

So you're more curb appeal to your mind is the full package from the curb through the driveway, through the walkway, through the front door, curb through the driveway, through the garage, all the way into the home.

The whole picture from start to finish. Is that correct?

Regina: "From the sidewalk to the backyard that's what we focus on, and like I said, making it very welcoming and even putting in a new welcome mat and maybe a cute plant next to it.

"And that's something we will provide if the house is vacant.

"I've had sellers say, 'Hey, I'm moving out of state. I don't have time to do all

that."

"We have vendors. We have landscaping, we have lawn care, repair, we have power washers.

We can do that for you, as far as the listing package.

"And even some staging, if the house is vacant and needs some staging, I definitely recommend that to my sellers."

So you can create a package for your sellers so where that your sellers effectively don't need to be there and you can take care of everything without any worry to your customers. As far as the curb appeal, the showing, the listing, the maintenance, and...

Regina: "Just the outside!"

Of course, you can handle the processes and the maintenance of the curb appeal maintenance while your customers can move on to the next home if they have to get over and start a new job somewhere else.

Is that correct?

Regina: "That is correct.

"I've had a lot of military families who had to relocate and there's here's the key to the house. They let me know what needs to be done. The cleaning curb appeal is all that we take care of for our sellers. If we're in that situation."

That's excellent to know. Is there anything else you'd like to talk about increasing your home's value?

Regina: "That was the exterior and then from the inside.

"Just if it's vacant, we'll get a professional housekeeping service to do a move-out cleaning, deep cleaning, they'll clean all the surfaces, they'll do the ovens, refrigerator, if there is one, all the things that people don't normally clean.

"We'll get somebody in there to clean it and make it nice.

"If it looks good, it smells good, people are going to want to live there.

"And if the seller is living there, we just I give them a list on how to declutter, to put things away that are controversial.

"I do recommend not having anything political, even family pictures lined out in their homes. Put all those personal things away, and just make it very neutral, very welcoming.

"Nothing personal left."

You want to make it as move-in ready for a visitor and potential buyer as possible. You want your buyers walking into your listings to see themselves immediately ready to move in.

Regina: "Correct.

"Correct, if they're living there, you know, they can start.

"That's one of some of the things that we tell them 21 days before it goes live sellers can start donating, trashing and, packing up things. Cleaning up things in the garage or closets. The closets are not too much of a big deal.

"If they open it, if it's cluttered, but just decluttering the surfaces that people are going to see as soon as they walk into the entire house."

I think I might be in trouble!

Is there anything else you'd like to add? I think we've hit the exterior and the interior.

Regina: "Yes, and it's going through the house. I will walk with the seller and just make those recommendations as needed."

The method of that, do you make an actual punch list like you might do for home building? Or is it specific?

Regina: "Correct. I do have a checklist for my sellers."

So it's a systematized process where we're not making it up every time as we go.

Regina: "Correct.

"And again, every home is unique.

"Every situation is different.

"So some of the pro tips may not apply, but I do hand them a checklist that will apply."

Outstanding. Anything else on the subject of home value?

Regina: "I think that's, I think we pretty much know that piece."

6 What Are The Costs Associated With Selling My Home?

What are, the costs associated with selling your home?

Regina: "Yeah, that's a big question for all sellers, right?

"That's what everybody wants to know.

"'How much is it going to cost me?'

"The cost of a real estate transaction. It could be different depending on the situation, with real estate.

"It used to be across the board where it was about, 6 to 8 percent for sellers scratch that I don't know if you heard about the lawsuits and all that.

"That's different, right?

"It's a little different nowadays since they're changing the real estate

concession pieces.

"So let me start over.

That's a good question because the cost of a real estate transaction includes concessions, closing costs, some repairs, some staging costs, and some title fees. All of that was out of the net proceeds of the property, and I outlined that for my sellers in a seller net sheet.

"If we're talking about concessions, the concession includes the realtor's negotiable commissions and also concessions that the seller might be willing to give for repairs or willing to give the buyer a concession for their closing costs.

"To answer your questions, the cost. Includes depends on the transaction commission closing costs for a seller could be about, I would say about 6. 5 to 7 percent because you have title fees.

"You have attorney fees, you have fees when you have some repair.

"It depends on the inspection report, and then you have the real estate concessions."

What are the most common repairs that are typically asked for? What are the three to five most common repairs that a buyer is going to ask a seller to make?

Regina: "The really three to four big ones are the roof, AC, water heater, foundation, and electrical box.

"That's five.

"Those are the most costly things that a buyer might have to endure once they take possession of the property.

"So once I look at the property for my sellers, we look at those structural changes. We notice any type of roof damage, the water heater, the AC, if they had any foundation problems.

"Especially if there are cracks on the walls. If there are doors that are sticking, and that could be a foundation issue.

"I look at the electrical box, so we address at least 5 of those, up front.

"And I let sellers know, 'Look, this

electrical box could be out of code. It's from the 70s. This could come up in the inspection report.' The seller will have to decide to either have it repaired, or give a concession to the buyer so he or she could do it after closing."

So we're going to try to get ahead of those things when we're listing.

Regina: "Yes.

"Realistically we have to, because you don't want a big surprise during the inspection report. That could be a deal breaker for some buyers and it causes the deal to terminate."

That's not what we want.

Regina: "Yeah, so the repairs could be big or they could be small.

"But the 5 main ones are the structure that I just mentioned.

"Small repairs, could be like, oh, the garage is not functioning. Or there's a

hole in the floor, or there's some things that need to be repaired.

"Keep in mind what an appraisal will want to look at. The appraiser will want to see surface-level things.

"They'll come in and look at if there's any wood rot. If there's wood rot, they'll call it out and say, 'This needs to be replaced before closing'.

"That's one of the common ones with VA loans. Conventional, they're a little bit more lenient.

"So termite damage, they're going to call it out. That's something that we need to get and repair."

So we want to hand over our home after the sale. We want our home in as quality a condition as possible before we even list. So we don't have those issues and negotiations and the risk of losing.

Regina: "If we're able to, yes.

"Sometimes there are things that we're not able to see the inspector will find. And then, it's a conversation that a seller. And I will talk about what they like to do.

"Typically, they have three choices when a repair and a repel amendment come to our table. We could either repair it, we can give a credit towards it, or we can reduce the price depending on

what it is."

If as a lister with you, I have a home and we suspect that we might have an issue, it's a minor issue, maybe chipped grout in a bathroom or an entryway. And it doesn't look serious. Is that something that you would be able to work with local contractors to get taken care of before inspections even start?

Or is that something that you would advise against?

Regina: "Oh, absolutely.

"If it's cosmetic, if it's very minor and cosmetic, then it's fine. Let's say the buyer wants to re-grout the whole house. But if it's something that's going to give it value, then yes, we have vendors.

"We have a handyman on our list that we can send over and get that repaired right away."

So again you're trying to make things as, as painless as possible for anyone who's listening with you.

Regina: "Correct."

Okay. Is there anything else that we'd like to hit associated with selling your home costs?

Regina: "Staging is an option. Some sellers like it. Some don't, just depending on what they think. There's also virtual staging we can do."

If you don't mind, what is staging?

Regina: "Good question.

"Staging is where a professional stager comes into the property and they can arrange your furniture and items to make it look very appealing.

"Or they can bring their items, their furniture, to furnish the house to make it very appealing.

"Statistics have shown that a stage home, or home with some furniture, sells faster than a vacant home."

So this connects in with your decluttering

suggestion and with the process of. Allowing buyers who are coming through the home to see things and be able to visualize what their furniture would look like in the home, as opposed to having completely vacant echoing walls.

Regina: "Yes, that's, yeah, that's the way of putting it."

Is there anything else you'd like to add?

Regina: "I think we nailed the costs associated with selling the home."

Outstanding.

7) How Long Sales Typically Take?

Let's talk about, how long it would typically take to sell a home in your experience, in the current markets versus difficult markets. What are the typical ranges? Of time that it takes to sell homes.

OPEN HOUSE | Saturday, February 4, 2023
1:00 - 3:00 pm

🛏 3 BEDS 🛁 2 BATHS 🏠 2,086 SQFT
5942 Lattimer Dr, Houston, TX | $380,000

Regina: "That can vary.

"That can vary depending on the factors. As I said, condition, pricing is the biggest, and right now the market

condition.

"With market conditions, like 2024 this year has been a little bit tougher, when you're not, then you're 20, 21, 22, 23.

"This is how it is.

"Market conditions have changed.

"Interest rates are higher. However, they have been steady.

"We keep a good eye on any changes that happen.

"So, I tell my sellers that if a home is priced right, the first two weeks on the market will tell us the story of where this home is going.

"If it's priced correctly, we'll have showings. I have had offers right then and there!

"If we don't, either it's priced too high, or just interest rates have spiked up and market conditions have changed.

"It's really hard to say to give a range, but typically a good home can sell within 30 to 60 days, priced correctly."

Is there a reason that one of your listers might choose to go with a very low home price in order to make their home move faster, to become more appealing?

Regina: "That has happened.

"We've had situations where there was distress in the home, not physically, but financially.

"They had to move it quickly.

"So they have had offers that were lower. They would take offers that are a little lower than what they wanted just to move it.

"But those are rare occasions. That doesn't really happen.

"For most sellers, my job is to get the

most money for the sellers, right?

"In cases where there is distress, either physically or financially, then I could see where a seller could lower the price a little bit just to get this done."

Let's take the, excuse me, let's take the other side of that. And if you have a home that's exceptionally positioned, it's a beautiful home, it's well, maintained, and It's in a it's a jewel.

New Price

308 Bennett Dr, West Columbia, TX
4 bed | 1 bath | 1,206 sqft | $1,250

And the seller's not particularly interested in selling. They're not a motivated seller.

What kind of pricing and what kind of listing techniques would we use for someone who's, doesn't need to sell, but wouldn't mind selling?

Regina: "That's definitely a unique situation.

"I just had that scenario earlier, this year.

"I had a gentleman who was selling his house. His house is in great condition, with original owners, lots of pride of ownership, beautiful home.

"And he had a price in mind as far as what he wanted. 'Not in a rush it's okay if it sits on the market'. He intentionally priced it high.

"Going against what I had recommended, which is fine.

"Again, he is the boss. I do what my

clients want me to do. We priced it at his price point.

"Thirty days later, we did a price reduction.

"So the first week we had two showings, no offers. Then the showings after week two kind of slowed down, and still no offers.

"We reduced the price. We had maybe one showing. The point is that when he priced it high, he intentionally did that because he was not in a hurry. Now the home sat there for a while and people were calling, asking, I was calling the neighbors and the neighbors were asking me like, 'What's going on? Why is this house sitting for 60 days'?

"It's unusual.

"What I recommended to my seller was to get the house appraised.

"He didn't want to get it appraised because he thought that what he had was in great condition, in a great location. Like you said, a hidden gem.

"The property sat there for 60 days.

"Finally, we agreed to lower the price to my recommendation.

"We had three offers right away. Even with my recommendations, they sent, we got under contract.

"He had an appraiser come in and it appraised. Because the comps didn't show exactly apples to apples, then they did a secondary appraiser appraisal that came in and did it.

"It met value just like I mentioned. Then his motivation was higher. It sped up whenever he saw that it sat there for 90 days. We got it closed in about 120 days."

Okay, so about. 30 days after the adjustment, we got to close.

Regina: "Yeah, about 60 days after the

adjustment. Yes."

Yes. Excuse me.

Regina: "60 days.

"So motivated sellers. Great.

"I do recommend if they want to get an appraisal done ahead of time, that's beneficial, but it's not necessary, against the comps.

"What I provide does show in the market will show because, at the end of the day, the buyers are what drive the price.

"I've had homes where the price had a cash offer. We sold it right away!

"This gentleman thought that his house should be appraised in a different neighborhood than where his neighborhood was based on the condition of his house.

"Took a little bit longer, but we got it

done."

What other aspects, other than the price and the setting of the home for sale, are the most useful methods to get your home once listed, sold other than price and setting.

Regina: "You broke out the last part. What was the question?"

Other than price, setting up a home, and doing the repairs for curb appeal purposes. What are the most important? Is there anything else that's really important? To help move your home and get yourself sold.

Regina: "Definitely available to, if you're occupying the property, be available for showings.

"Showings are very important and also as an agent, communicate over and over. Communicate from both sides. From my side to the sellers and the sellers to me. I like that communication to be open the whole entire transaction.

"So we're, there's no question about

what's going on with the home. I think that's very important to get it done."

Is there anything else that you'd like to add about selling your home? The time it takes to sell your home, excuse me.

Regina: "We also look at the market.

"I provide a market data sheet every week.

"So based on the market, that might be changing again with the new interest rate and some of the new rules that we're getting from NAR. Then days on the market could be a little bit longer, but I keep again, communication with my sellers about any changes weekly in the market in their area."

8) What Should I Expect During The Sales Process?

What should I, as a lister of my home, expect during the sales process from start to start? Of the listing date all the way through close. What's my, what's my timeline? What should I expect out of you as my listing agent? And how do we, how do we go through the process of the sale?

Regina: "Definitely communication.

Just like we talked about, you will hear from me constantly that 'over-communicating' is the key.

"I'll walk you through the process of how to set your home up 21 days prior. We use a 21-day campaign where we can put the home is coming soon on the MLS. Thanks. And that 21 days, it'll give you the time, it'll give the sellers the time to get the seller's disclosure filled out, warranties, any repairs, any curb appeal done.

"Once the home is active on the market, we'll start hosting the showings.

"A seller will receive an email as well as a text message with any showing appointments. And they can approve it or deny it. They'll come to me, either approve it or deny it.

"First two weeks is where they'll tell us how the home is doing. We have a lot of showings. We're doing well. If we don't,

then that means that we have to rethink our strategy.

"In week three, we do an open house. If the home is not under contract, the open house will be done on Saturday from one to three.

"We will invite all of the neighbors.

"That's another thing.

"I call the neighbors and invite all of them to our open house.

"I'll call any showing agent that has come in and maybe want to bring their buyers for the second time.

"We call, we make it very inviting. We have fresh cookies. We have drinks. We make it very nice for the neighbors to come in and see, what the seller is selling.

"A lot of them are nosy neighbors, but we still, 'Hey, come on. You might have a friend that wants to buy it'!

"If we receive an offer, then I present every single offer to the seller, no matter what the price is. Low offer, same good offer, high offer. I send it in an email form, we discuss it, we talk about it, and if we accept it, we negotiate.

Once we negotiate and send it for execution, it goes to the title.

In the beginning, the seller will fill out some of the paperwork and they need to expect some fees, like HOA, if there's an HOA. Sellers will have some paperwork they'll have to do on their end at first.

"The first 7 days, 7 to 10 days, is what we call the option period. This is where sellers have allowed the buyers to take the house off the market for 7 days as an option period to get it inspected or they can change their mind for whatever reason.

"That option period, if the buyer decides to terminate, they're able to do then we just put it back on the market. If the option period goes well, with nothing major coming up, we still negotiate repairs, we negotiate in that period for the best interest of the seller.

"If we continue with the pending contract, then the lender will order an appraisal. The appraisal can take about 10 days. The lender will do most of the lifting at that time to get the buyer to be qualified, and then to the closing table.

"But for every step that we receive from title, anything that lenders require, I communicate that with my seller. So they know exactly what's going on every single week. And sometimes no news is good news, especially within the option period. That option period can, as I said, the buyer can terminate for any reason if they like, and then they'll get their earnest money back.

"And then the seller gets to keep the option fee, which is normally a couple hundred dollars."

Is there anything else you'd like to add?

Regina: "When we get to the closing, I definitely advise my clients on how to get to the closing table by turning in keys, turning off utilities, and just getting it ready to turn over to the next owner."

9) What Are The Potential Risks & Challenges?

What are the potential risks and challenges that are most common? What are the five or 10 most common risks and challenges that you've seen for your customers while listing?

Regina: "Good question.

"We've had, with this hot market, we've had a lot of low offers from investors.

"I work with a lot of investors, and they're great.

"But whenever we're trying to sell a home, if it's an investment home, a lot of investors try to send lowball offers. And there are times that these offers are so low that sometimes it's not even, worth it.

"I tell my sellers, 'Hey, if you don't want me to present offers lower than this amount, I won't.'

"So, low offers are one.

"Financing issues with buyers have happened. If they're using financing, such as a lender, there, there's some things that they need to do that square themselves away. And then also unexpected repairs, but we try to get ahead of the repair, so it's not a surprise to the seller.

"That's what my job is to make sure that we mitigate the risk, in pricing that correctly and also getting ahead of the curve for the repairs that might come."

It sounds like the three most common issues are, they're major issues, but this sounds like we can mitigate almost all of those with planning and the systems that we have in place.

Regina: "Correct.

"Now we try to screen our buyers as much as possible and address any type of issues.

"Quickly, however, some buyers can not get financing.

"That's one of the biggest risks!

"When you see a house go back on the market it is either because of inspection - repairs, or because the buyer couldn't get financing. So, the buyer not getting financing hurts the seller because now you took the home off the market. It can even be off the market for 30 days before the financing falls apart.

"That hasn't happened to me.

"We try to vet out the buyers very well by calling the lender, asking them good questions about, debt to racial income. Asking about credit score. Asking if there are any contingencies. If they have enough money for closing costs. If they have enough money for down payment. And making sure that they're well vetted.

"Now, pre-approval is required for every transaction. Sometimes it's just on a piece of paper.

"Some agents may not do their due diligence and reach out to their agent, the buyer's agent, and the lender.

"I try to call them and get as many questions answered as possible, so we're not facing a financial risk down the line."

If I recall, when my parents retired, they had a home buyer for their home, which is a larger home in the Northeast, and their process was about 45 days. And the buyer broke out and 1 of the issues was that the buyer on who was under contract failed to pay. The retainer, the contract, and the contracted retainer for the home. Has that ever happened to you? And how would you mitigate something like that?

Regina: "They failed to pay the retainer?

I may be using the wrong word, but there was a contract, a down payment basically

Regina: "Okay. The payment"

Home and they failed. They brought in a when the buyers broke out the contract, they effectively wasted the, my parents, the listing. The lister's time by failing to go through with the contract, they made it all the way through the contract.

And the buyers walked away from the lister at the closing table. And it was basically 45 or 60 days of wasted listing time. how does that kind of,

Regina: "That hasn't happened to me.

"**We haven't had that.**

"**Only time we had a similar situation whenever the home, was through a loan and then the lender had to switch loans in the middle of it from a FHA to a conventional one. That was actually minor error. Because she was here on a visa, and there was a misspelling of her name that didn't match.

"So the lender was like, 'We're not giving out the loan'. So then the lender canceled.

"I haven't had any contingencies like that, they have to sell a home. It doesn't sell that can't happen.

"In fact, I have a listing right now that we were very close to accepting an offer with a 90-day contingency, where the buyer had to put their home for sale and it didn't sell or she hasn't put it on the market yet.

"She thinks he home will sell in 90 days, but she's asking us to take our listing off the market until October.

"But there's a 50 / 50 chance that her house may or may not sell!

"So we were about to accept that offer. My client was fine with it, but my recommendation was that 'we will do that, but we will continue to show our

your listed home, so you could still do an option pending. Then we continue to show if there's a contingency where fine, we have a contract, but just know that if there is another contract that comes since your house hasn't sold that we can take that contract'.

If that makes sense."

Absolutely. It's an option, a purchase option. Would cover,

Regina: "An option."

A purchase option would cover and not waste your lister's time.

Regina: "Yes.

"Because again, if you're still continuing to show it, people can still make appointments, come see the property, and possibly have an option to sell a better offer."

So someone comes to your lister, makes an offer, and they're not ready to close immediately. They basically have a first right of refusal option.

Regina: "There is a form, we do have a form for that.

"You contingency that could blow up the deal, but, being with Shaw Real Estate for 4 years, our philosophy is we take everything to the mat. We close everything we touch because we try to mitigate the risk. We try to just get ahead of the curve and get everything with no surprises and then get it to the closing table.

"That's what he always says. We got to take it to the mat and we got to take it to the closing table."

<u>10) Strong Process To Vet Buyers</u>

So you've mentioned, you have mentioned vetting your buyers several times. It sounds like you've got a very strong process to go through vetting buyers. Is that true?

Regina: "That is true.

"We, as I mentioned before, reach out to the lender and we get pre-approval.

"Because nowadays, anybody can get a pre-approval letter online and submit an offer!

"We have to be careful and mindful of the lender that they're using and who's sending the pre-approval. When we go in and call, we make sure that it is a reputable mortgage company or lender.

"It could be national, it could be local. As long as we get somebody on the phone make sure we ask those questions. Like I was mentioning, the debt to income ratio, the down payment, if they have enough money to close, if there are any contingencies.

That is all very important!

"Even in a multiple-offer scenario, if we have several offers on the table, I will call each one of those lenders, to get more information on that pre-approval letter and on the buyers."

Is there anything else that you, is there anything else involved in the vetting process that you do?

Regina: "Yeah.

"I also try to really communicate with the buyer's agent to see how well they know their buyers.

"If they make sure that they're also done their homework to make sure that they're qualified. If he or she knows the answer about not necessarily their credit score, but if they know there are any contingencies, that's a racial income. If they have a good communication with the lender.

"Because a buyer's agent works very hand in hand with the lender. Buyer's agent will know the pre-approval process, the conditional approval process, and the clear to close before I will ever know.

"They get the communication first and then I'm always asking, but I also reach

out to the lender myself before just listening to the buyer's agent.

"And if we haven't gotten clear to close by a certain time, why not talk to me about what's going on? We need to get this close."

So we're going, so as my listing agent, you're going to actively engage with the buyers and the financing institutions. In order to make sure that we're moving things forward on a timely basis.

Regina: "Yes, absolutely.

"Communicating with the buyer's agent and the lender is part of what I do.

"It's my job to do so for the best interest of my sellers."

I understand. Is there anything else you'd like to add to that?

Regina: "I think we're good."

11) How Do You Handle Offers & Negotiations?

All right. How do you handle offers and negotiations then? Because we've worked through the listing process. Obviously, we're going to need offers and negotiations. What's, what are the main components we're looking for when we get into the offer phase?

Regina: "So when we get offers we present them to our clients and each offer is different, right?

"Just because we have the highest offer doesn't mean it's the best offer!

"This means if we have three offers, one's high, one that's at the listing, or two are at the listing, then the high offer is not necessarily the best offer for my sellers.

"What I like to do is when I present an offer we don't just base it on price.

"It's also important in the terms.

"Price is important, of course, the most money want to get the most money for the seller. But the terms of the offer are important for my sellers.

"If there's something that they need to adhere to, for example, if my seller needs it, if they're living in the home, they may need a lease back. This means that they need to stay in the home a little bit longer after closing, and then we try to negotiate a free lease back for sellers.

"So that gives our seller a little bit of time to get their funds. To schedule the movers to be able to move out a week or two later.

"I've had that happen!

"A Marine Corps buddy of ours sold his house.

"He was moving to New Jersey. He needed a 30-day lease back.

"Most of the time buyers will charge rent, will charge a fee for our seller to stay after close.

"We negotiated a free 30-day lease back for him.

"The terms as far option period, shorter option period. Some can wait for contingency. Some can wait for appraisals. Being in the driver's seat with, my sellers, when I receive an offer,

we stay firm and we make sure that we drive that offer up again, not necessarily just on price, but on terms for my seller."

So it sounds based upon some of what you mentioned earlier, that the most of, one of the most valuable tools you have for getting a quality price with good terms is having multiple offers come in on listings you're doing for your customers. Does that sound about right?

Regina: "That's correct.

"And even if I have one offer on the table, we go back to the drawing board and we negotiate, like I said, more favorable terms to my buyer, to my seller.

"Each situation is unique.

"It's different.

"And sometimes the seller says, 'Just take the offer and accept the terms'.

"I definitely respect that, they're the

boss, but I recommend getting a little bit more for your bang for your buck. So they like the offer why not a shorter option period? If they lock the offer, that's fine.

"Let's negotiate during the repair period, the option period, meaning we accepted the buyer's offer. Our sellers are happy with it. Repairs come, asking for either a concession or they're asking for a price reduction.

"I say 'Stay firm'.

"We try to, again, mitigate that risk at the beginning, so my seller's shocked at what they're asking for. But again, we stay, I stay firm for our seller."

Understood. Is there anything else you'd like to add to offers and negotiations?

Regina: "No, I've had every scenario you can think of.

"So if there's a negotiation or a situation, I probably had it.

"I guess what I'm trying to say is that I have expertise in that negotiation piece and any situation."

12 What Else Sets You Apart From Other Realtors?

So it sounds like you're extremely experienced. You've got an exceptional follow-up process and you have. Systems in place to benefit your listing families. What else sets you apart from other realtors?

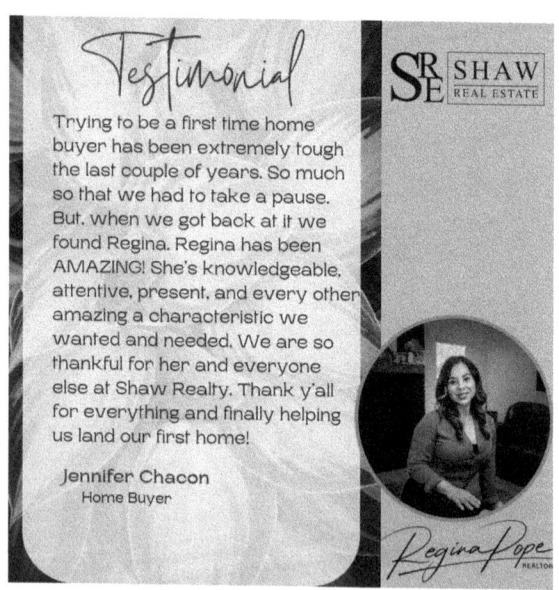

Regina: "I treat everybody like family to me, it's more than just a transaction and I always value relationships. Because, to me, helping a seller in any given situation is helping them solve a problem.

Whether it is moving out of state, families change all the time, family dynamics change, or life situations change.

"I try to be there to smooth everything over and help them get to that closing table. And I feel like building that rapport and having that relationship with them, again, treating them like family versus just a transaction has been very strong, has created a very strong relationship with people where I've gotten a lot of referrals just for that.

"I want all my sellers to say, 'Yeah, Regina she's understanding, but she's good. She's firm and she's helped us solve a problem'.

"I guess that's my biggest focus.

"How can I help you solve a problem to get you to achieve your goal."

How do you personalize your approach for each family who lists their home with you?

Regina: "Question and everybody's unique.

"So most realtors will go in and they'll do the same thing. They'll bring comps that they already looked at If they have a listing presentation, they'll go in with comps.

"They'll go in with a price in mind, right? Yes?

"You do your homework prior, but again, I go in there just to try to solve the situation so if a seller's just went through something like a divorce or death in the family. I helped them with that.

"Maybe that probate process or make sure that they have their ducks in the road, who gets awarded the house during the divorce. Or maybe a situation where there's a job relocation.

"I can take the brunt of the work to help them get the house ready.

"Again, it's very unique.

"It's hard to say if there's like a system in place.

"All my systems are the same, but it's unique to that person."

So you're customizing systems to people's individual needs and adapting as you're listing customer needs. How do you do it?

Regina: "Correct, I've had sellers for,

they've had zero money for repairs.

"They need to sell for financial situations.

"I have a handyman. I have people who I can call and sometimes I have to take that and, pay out of my pocket for them to get the house sold.

"So they can have that money for whatever situation that they need, so there, there's been a lot of unique things I've done for my sellers.

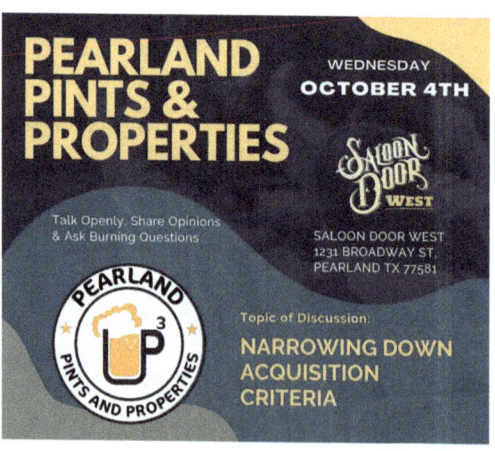

"I take pride in that because it's helping people. It's not just a transaction."

Is there anything else that you'd like to add?

Regina: "I think we covered almost everything. Do you have any questions for me?"

No, just to wrap things up. I know that you had mentioned in a prior conversation that you had, You had a different kind of listing that you had taken care of today. What other services do you offer potential clients that they might be interested in? Not necessarily with the listing process, but later on in life.

Regina: "Yeah, so we are a full brokerage that offers residential, buying, and selling, as well as investing.

"We are part of Parallel Plants and Property.

"I work with a lot of investors who are trying to grow their portfolios. Whether, they want to grow their portfolios or they want to, sell and buy something bigger.

"Also commercial.

"I have been dabbling in commercial real estate a lot lately.

"We have several listings where we have the day we have daycare owners. I have law firms, and flower shops. We have several businesses.

"Again, they're just people trying to solve a problem.

"And we've we have been helping a lot of buyers. And sellers for commercial properties as well."

Are you selling the full business or are you selling the location itself?

Regina: "We can do both. We can sell the business location together or separately."

Okay, what about, let's talk a little bit more about the investments because you mentioned that a few times during our conversation.

Regina: "Yeah.

"The goal is for investors to grow their portfolios.

"We work with several that want to either buy and flip or buy and hold whatever their needs are. We have, access to a lot of market properties. We're part of this group called Pines and Properties and we will find off-market deals for investors that want to grow there.

"A lot of them don't want to go through the MLS because of some of the multiple offers and this and that. They want to get good deals so they can be profitable.

"My broker, started as an investor when he got out of the Marine Corps and bought his first property, renovated it flipped it, and sold it. And he has a really intensive spreadsheet and formula that he can use for any investor that's trying to grow.

"We have an investor who's trying to sell a couple of properties to buy multi-multifamily.

"We have a lady who has 60 doors and owns apartment buildings and not also that we help her buy and sell those we also offer property management. If she needs, if any investor, we need that as well."

So you have a full suite of services. You can buy and sell residential homes, plus you've got access to investor portfolios for both buying and selling. And you can operate into the business transactions, buying and selling businesses along with the real estate and the dirt that they're sitting on.

Regina: "Correct."

Are there any other services other than the tenant management that you offer?

Regina: "No, property management, like you mentioned, and leasing.

"I have some of my investors become landlords and I help them lease their properties I also help buyers. I do have a team member that does the buyers and the leases.

"For me, I focus mainly on sellers and then commercials, but we do, if there's somebody who is looking for a rental, we can help."

Conclusion:

Is there anything else that you'd like to add before we start wrapping up?

Regina: "Yes, you can find me on social media and reginapope.com, on our website and on, on HAR."

Outstanding. Anything else you'd like to throw in?

Regina: "Oh, thank you so much for having me on. I enjoy this."

Glad to have you. We'll we'll wrap up now.

Regina: "Thank you."

ABOUT THE AUTHOR

Doug Franklin is husband, father, US Army Combat Infantry Officer, serial entrepreneur, BJJ practitioner, social media Luddite, marketing, SEO & AdWords expert, math nerd with LSSBB & PMP certifications, and an occasional book scribbler, I mean author.

Regina has been a friend for about six years at the time of writing. Years ago we discussed how my business book helped my home improvement business and determined Regina needed her own. Unfortunately, it has taken entirely too long to bring this volume into reality.

If you are interested in your own business book or another project to help your business, I really enjoy creative endeavors to help people grow their businesses. Please check out the ABOUT page for more information about your own EXPERT SALES PROFESSIONAL book:

www.ingramcontent.com/pod-product-compliance
Lightning Source LLC
Chambersburg PA
CBHW070159230526
45471CB00002B/733